Sarah,
I hope this blesses
+ encourages you!
~Natalie

Jesus.
Yoga Pants.
Homeschool.

Dr. Natalie Trent Bruce

Copyright © 2018 Dr. Natalie Trent Bruce.

All rights reserved. No part of this book may be used or reproduced by any means, graphic, electronic, or mechanical, including photocopying, recording, taping or by any information storage retrieval system without the written permission of the author except in the case of brief quotations embodied in critical articles and reviews.

Scripture taken from the King James Version of the Bible

WestBow Press books may be ordered through booksellers or by contacting:

WestBow Press
A Division of Thomas Nelson & Zondervan
1663 Liberty Drive
Bloomington, IN 47403
www.westbowpress.com
1 (866) 928-1240

Because of the dynamic nature of the Internet, any web addresses or links contained in this book may have changed since publication and may no longer be valid. The views expressed in this work are solely those of the author and do not necessarily reflect the views of the publisher, and the publisher hereby disclaims any responsibility for them.

Any people depicted in stock imagery provided by Getty Images are models, and such images are being used for illustrative purposes only. Certain stock imagery © Getty Images.

ISBN: 978-1-9736-4395-1 (sc)
ISBN: 978-1-9736-4394-4 (e)

Library of Congress Control Number: 2018912907

Print information available on the last page.

WestBow Press rev. date: 11/05/2018

To Reagan, my encourager,
who taught me how to be a mom
when I didn't know if I was cut out for the job.

To Travis, my rock, who supports me
no matter what crazy journey I decide to take.

To my Mom, my cheerleader, who
always believes in me.

Contents

Introduction 1
1 The Calling 5
2 Finding Your Why 11
3 Fear Debunking 19
4 Jesus. Yoga Pants. Homeschool. 25
5 The Curriculum Quandary 29
6 Step One: Community 33
7 Step Two: Creating YOUR Homeschool 37
8 Step Three: The Home-Field Trip Balance 45
9 Exposure Learning 51
10 Scheduling and Structure 59
11 Homeschooling Your High Schooler 65
12 A Word of Encouragement 73
About the Author 77

Introduction

This is not the story I had planned. With my Masters in Counseling and Doctorate in Educational Leadership, I envisioned myself making a difference to a lot of people. I envisioned a fancy office, lunch breaks, and using the bathroom without a toddler sitting on my lap. I expected paid vacations, promotions, and being referred to by my colleagues as Dr. Bruce instead of "MOMMMMMMMM!" I had a plan that was well thought out, full of achievement, and selfish. I also had a pretty average and privileged life, not rendering itself to much of a testimony. I always wanted to have some sort of testimony I could share. Then I got it.

There is nothing like motherhood to break you and make you look at life with a fresh perspective. My entire testimony is my motherhood journey. God took this selfish, career driven woman who lived for vacations and molded her into a homeschooling, stay-at-home mom. The dress code isn't as glamorous, the pay is nonexistent, but the benefits…Thank You, Lord. Thank You for giving me the opportunity to look at life and see what really matters. Thank You for giving me the ability to stay home with my children so they could teach me how to be a mother. Thank You for opening my heart to Your calling to keep them at home with me throughout their school years. Watching them grow up and learn about Your world is a privilege.

It is also a choice. Choosing to stay home with your children for an extended number of years is a sacrifice of yourself. You sacrifice part of your income, and the extras that went along with that income. Your way of life may change due to less finances, such as a smaller home, older car, hand-me-down clothes, and couponing. Your vacations may be fewer or closer to home. Your heart may sometimes ache for adult conversation, recognition, or accomplishment.

But your accomplishment is right in front of you. You are making a difference in the lives of your children, and the potential for the impact of their lives is limitless. Live with no regrets, my friends. And I promise you, you will never regret spending time with your children. You will never regret investing in them.

Shortly after the birth of our oldest child, my husband's work relocated us to a new town. I felt isolated and lonely, strangely lonelier with a new baby, I suppose because my life and schedule revolved around her. I was an unintentional stay-at-home mom due to my husband's relocation, and not feeling fulfilled in that role.

We started attending a small church, where I met a friend who has had more of an impact on my life in the one year we lived in that town together than she probably realizes. She was a mom of four. That in itself made no sense to me. Having one child made me feel like I was treading water and never quite enough. I asked her about it one day. I said, "Don't you feel like with each child you have there is less and less love to go around?" She replied with a joyful smile, "No, it is actually the opposite. Each child we have has that many more siblings to love them. So really, each child has been loved so much more." It made sense, but I didn't fully understand it until I had my second child. Then my third. If God blesses us with more, I know I will be reminded of my friend's wisdom.

She always seemed so content. More than content, really, she seemed so joyful in her role as a wife and mother. She frequently volunteered at church events and stayed busy homeschooling her four children. She would sometimes ask me if I ever considered homeschooling. I would dodge the question by saying we had several more years before we would have to think about school. I would mention it to my husband in the evenings and we would laugh together. No way would we homeschool. Once our kids were in school, I would return to my work. I even asked my friend once, "Aren't you worried your kids will turn out weird if they are homeschooled?" She confidently answered, "Oh, homeschool kids are only weird if their parents are weird." I now ponder what exactly that means for my own kids.

This is our story. A story about a family that never intended to homeschool. A story of God calling us to something we didn't want to do, with a list of fears and doubts to back us up. Then our story changed. We became a homeschool family. It's more than school, really. Homeschooling is a way of life. It's spending time together, finding learning opportunities in everyday activities. It's giving your child the gift of time, teaching them to slow down and be present. It's less technology and more play. It's teaching your child how to learn, and to love learning.

My intention behind this book is that you could be considering homeschooling today, read this book after you put the kids to bed tonight, and be encouraged to step out in faith tomorrow to begin your homeschool journey. My hope is that our story helps you find (or reignite) your passion for homeschooling.

1
The Calling

I always wondered what people meant when they said, "God called us to homeschool." I was certain God would never call me to that. No, God was calling me to drop my kids off at school, meet some friends for breakfast at Panera, then go home and take a nap. That is what I deserved after being in the trenches of child-rearing for the better part of a decade. I would eventually return to work, but first I needed to rest.

Then, God called us to homeschool. We didn't give in willingly. His nudges were subtle and gradual, and we persistently denied the need to make such a drastic change to our plans. Our plans were good plans. They didn't need changing. But like so many times in our parenting journey, God took us on a ride we never planned to take. I was embarrassed at first. When people would ask my daughter what grade she was in or what school she attended, she would proudly announce, "My mommy is my mommy teacher!" I would feel my face getting hot. We had just been outed as social outcast weirdos. But I've got to tell you…*I am loving it.*

Our journey to homeschool started with our oldest daughter attending public preschool. She had previously attended a Christian preschool two mornings a week beginning at 9:00am, and thrived in that environment. But when we were given the opportunity for her to attend public preschool, her attitude toward school quickly changed. At the age of four, she was now going to school four mornings a week, beginning at 7:45am. She began crying every morning on our way to school, saying she didn't like school and she was afraid she would be hurt by her classmates.

After meeting with her teacher, we discovered her class was made up of several students varying in academic and developmental ability. It was difficult for the teacher to see everything that was going on in the class, and was not aware of our daughter's struggles. Our hope was that preschool would continue to foster her love for learning and friendship, and encourage her to grow academically as she was approaching kindergarten. Instead, she was seemingly regressing both socially and academically, no longer enjoyed learning, and was afraid of going to school.

We decided this was not setting the educational tone we intended to set as we were preparing for kindergarten.

We wanted our daughter to start kindergarten with joy in her heart, ready to make new friends and learn new things. Public preschool seemed to be doing more harm than good, and at this point she was now terrified of all school settings including the Christian preschool she enjoyed so much. So, we decided to take a break. Maybe with time, she would forget about all this and we could start fresh with kindergarten. We were still not considering homeschooling at this point, rather just taking a break.

This is where God started calling. I would hear parents talk about things that were going on in their child's elementary class. Things like: running isn't allowed at recess; talking isn't allowed at lunch; skipping is prohibited because it is unsafe; my daughter doesn't seem to be learning very much; I don't see my son all day, and when he gets home we have an hour of homework to complete; we are always in a rush to get to school, get to our extra-curriculars, eat dinner quickly, get homework done, get a bath, get to bed to make sure we are rested to start all over again the next morning to rush to get to school. Everything seemed to focus around school. Life, starting at the age of five, revolved around school. And while we are sending our children away for the better part of the day, what are they really learning in those eight hours?

I continued to protest. No, Lord. I am not cut out to homeschool. There are some mothers that are meant to homeschool, but I am not one of them. My patience is short, and the idea of teaching a child how to read sounds about as easy as flying to the moon. I have some serious concerns about me as a homeschooler, and those concerns are growing into a long list of fears. And what about my life? My fantasy about sending my kids to school, and everything I could do during that time like take a nap, or clean my house, or go back to work! What about my work, Lord? I have all of this school loan debt. How can I pay that off when I am homeschooling my kids?

I eventually conceded to just give it a try. It wasn't going to work out, I just knew it. But, when God is calling you to do something, the least you can do is give it your Girl Scout try so you can say, "Hey God, I tried!" It was a Monday morning. My kids were watching tv. I had bought some school materials and had made a plan of what our first "lesson" would be about. It was the letter A. We were going to practice writing it in a sand tray, talk about the sound the letter A makes, and list words starting with the letter A. I had a cute craft planned of a letter A that looked like an alligator. Next week, I told myself, next week I will give homeschooling a try and we will learn about the letter A.

Next week? But I have all of my supplies, and my lesson ready to go! Let's just do this! My voice was literally trembling as I said, "Reagan, would you like to turn off the tv and come in the kitchen and do school with me?" I think I thought my four-year-old was going to tell me to buzz off and turn the tv up to drown out my voice. Instead, she yelled, "Yeah!" Our lesson lasted about forty-five minutes. We had so much fun learning about the letter A. At the end I asked if she wanted to learn about the letter B tomorrow, and she said she did! By the end of the week, we were a homeschool family.

Day one of homeschooling. Learning about the letter A.

I realized that what takes eight hours to accomplish in a classroom of students varying in learning styles and developmental abilities, could be accomplished at home in one to three hours (depending on age) of uninterrupted activity targeted to meet your child where they are. Meeting my child where she was, academically and socially, quickly reduced her anxiety and increased her confidence.

At the beginning, I thought of homeschooling as something we would do when our children were young. Homeschool maybe through elementary school, then send them to public school for middle and high school. But it didn't take long for me to fall in love with homeschooling. Suddenly the list of reasons why I love homeschooling were much longer than the original list of fears and doubts I had. I will always leave room for God's plan and the different needs of each of my children, but at this point, I can't see myself giving up on homeschooling. I have become a full-blown lover of this life.

2
Finding Your Why

Why do I homeschool? This question can be answered in my heart by reminiscing about a random Thursday last Spring. We drove to a town two hours away to meet some old friends that had moved away. We met them at a children's science center. Our kids played together all day, picking up right where they had left off several months prior. We packed a sack lunch and spent most of the day there. I loved catching up with my friend from back home, while watching my kids make all sorts of hands-on discoveries. Their favorite part of the science center was the earth quake simulator. They would all stand as a small group on a square, and it would begin to rumble and shake, and they would all scream and run off of it.

Our friends had to return home to pick their oldest child up from school, but we stayed a few more hours until we were worn out from exploring the entirety of the science center. We were hungry for dinner, and this town had one of our favorite restaurants that our town didn't have. I ordered my favorite, and the kids felt like royalty with gourmet macaroni and cheese and raspberry lemonade. Then, giant chocolate cake for dessert. We sat and ate and visited about the day, talking about how much fun we had with our friends, and all of the cool discoveries we had made and new things we had learned.

During that meal, my daughter asked, "Mom, who created God?" Then my son piggy backed her question with his own, "Mom, did God make ants?" We discussed the answers to their questions thoughtfully. On the car ride home, with everyone passed out in the back seat, I realized what a gift it was to homeschool my children. Their faith has the capacity to grow so quickly in these early years, and they have so many questions. Who better to be there to listen to and answer these questions than mom or dad? I wondered if they would have even had the time to ponder those questions if they were caught up in the hustle and bustle of a busy school day. And if they did ponder those questions at school, who would have answered them? And how would they have been answered?

That great day is my perfect example of homeschooling. We had the flexibility to fellowship with old friends in the middle of the week. We spent the day learning through unstructured hands-on play. We ate chocolate cake. And most importantly, we had the time to explore our curiosities about God together. I can't think of anything better.

I believe in homeschooling. In fact, I have to watch myself because I have become so passionate about homeschooling that I am bordering on proud. I have done a total 180. I used to mumble under my breath with an ashamed tone of voice, "we homeschool." Now I announce it to anyone that will listen, "We Homeschool!" That change of heart is due to my why. Everyone has to have their why. It is what will drive you to jump on this journey, and stay on it when the road gets rocky. People will often ask you why you homeschool, but more importantly than having an answer for them, you need to know the answer for yourself.

I would encourage you to spend some quiet time pondering what it is you really want out of this season of life. What do you really want? That question can be a hard one to ask yourself, because what we really want out of life often takes sacrifice and requires the harder road over the easier road. The road less traveled has huge rewards throughout it, but it can get bumpy.

Once you can answer that question for yourself, think of what you are doing to help you get what you want, and what areas you need to make a change in. During my time of contemplation about homeschooling,

I visited with a mother who homeschooled her five children from birth through graduation. All of those children are grown and gone now. As we talked and I shared my heart with her about what I wanted for my children I said, "Everyday, I pray over my children that they will grow to know God, love God, and serve God." She replied, "In regard to school, what path do you believe will most encourage your children to know, love, and serve God?"

> Train up a child in the way he should go, and when he is old he will not depart from it.
> Proverbs 22:6

Since mainstream public school became common practice in America, the decision for a family to homeschool was often rooted in fear. This fear stemmed from the idea that God was being removed from education, which would contribute to moral standards among teachers and students to slip. If our children were spending the majority of their time not learning about God, or furthermore learning contradictions to God, and socializing with children whose moral compass was off track, what would become of our children? Would they adopt a poor moral compass? Would God slowly play a less important role in their lives, or possibly be replaced with other ideas?

This fear often manifested itself in public school bashing. Homeschooling was a better decision than sending our children to that terrible school down the road that was no doubt filled with godless people trying to corrupt my angel. In reality, the school down the road may very well be filled with well-intentioned Christian teachers and administrators that love on and care for their students very well. So, basing our decision to homeschool solely on the reaction to fear isn't totally accurate, and may not be setting us up for homeschool success.

Intrinsic motivation, or motivation that comes from within us, will always drive us to accomplish more and do our best. Extrinsic motivation, or motivation driven by external forces, often dies short of completion or is completed just to get it done. Extrinsic motivation takes the joy out of what you are accomplishing. Homeschooling just because you don't like the public school system may not produce the same fruit as homeschooling because you love homeschooling.

The fear of our children becoming of the world because they are in the world has led some to a decision to homeschool. Increasing our control equals decreasing the likelihood that we lose them. The decision to homeschool at that point is reactive to fear. While this motive to homeschool still exists today, we see many other motives playing an important role in the decision to homeschool. These motives are more proactive than reactive. Proactive toward giving our children as many opportunities as possible to experience childhood and learn within the constructs of a loving, Christian community.

Homeschooling is a proactive mode of teaching and modeling life principles that will stick with our children for their lifetime. This can be done through learning measurements while helping mom cook a meal for a neighbor in need of a blessing. Or talking about kindness when sibling rivalry rears up. Or serving as a family in the local mission field. Or stopping in the middle of an intense math lesson to pray for patience and an open mind.

With every child I have, I feel the clock ticking faster. Suddenly they are five years old, and the amount of waking time we have with them has the potential to get cut by two-thirds when we send them off to school. And during the third that they are ours, we need to squeeze homework into the lineup of dinner, bath, and the overabundance of American extra-curriculars that busy our lives. I wasn't ready to give up that time. I wasn't ready to introduce my child to the rush and busyness of life. That will inevitably come, but not yet.

There are so many reasons to homeschool today. Not reasons reactive to fear, or extrinsically motivated by public school bashing. But reasons proactive toward the life you want to offer your child, an investment in their entire life. More than anything, it's giving your child the gift of time. Time to learn. Time to ask questions. Time to be with family. Time to explore. Time to rest. Time to struggle. Time to serve. Time to mourn. Time to play. Time to eat. Time to pray. Time to make mistakes. Time to discover what they enjoy and are good at. Time to realize what is really important.

3
Fear Debunking

God's calling or not, I had a laundry list of fears as long as my arm. Every time I thought of just one of those fears, that was enough for me to label this idea as ridiculous and enroll my daughter in kindergarten. After all, that is what everyone does. They enroll their child in kindergarten. How bad could it really be? My husband and I were public schooled, and we turned out fine!

However, school isn't what it was thirty years ago when I was in school. Technology alone has completely changed education. Some of that change is very helpful. Yet, some of that change puts an iPad in the hands of every kindergarten student and is teaching them through visual and auditory stimulation that will make reading chapter books someday virtually unbearable. Many schools aren't teaching cursive anymore, and learning to read using the phonics system has taken a backseat to memorizing sight words. Children are being taught based on what they will be tested on, and this has changed the way teachers teach. Combine this with the change in social climate related to bullying, a breakdown in the family unit, technology doing most of the parenting, and a culture that is removing God from our value system, and public school was becoming less and less of an option for our family. But my fear of homeschooling continued to haunt me.

I made a list of all my fears. I talked this list over with as many homeschool moms as I could find. I was especially interested in veteran moms who were now at the end of their homeschool journey and could share their joys, their regrets, and give me any advice they had learned along the way. Here is my list of fears, along with debunks for each.

- **What if I can't teach my child to read?** Your child actually has more potential as a reader in a homeschool environment that teaches phonics, has read-aloud time, visits the library frequently, and values reading time for learning as well as enjoyment. A reading resource that I highly recommend once your child has learned their letters and letter sounds is *Bob Books* by Bobby Lynn Maslen.
- **What if our personalities clash?** Some days they will. This offers ample opportunity for conflict

resolution within the constructs of your home, which will prepare them for conflict later in life. Some days you will need to take a break from school because emotions are running high, and that can be a great time to pray together.

- **What happens when my child's math ability surpasses mine?** When you are no longer able to teach your child math concepts or are unable to assist them with concepts taught in their curriculum set, hire a tutor, enroll them in an online course, or depending on their age, enroll your child in a dual credit college math course.
- **How can I teach my child things I don't even know?** Much of homeschooling is you, as the parent and teacher, modeling learning and a love for learning. It won't take long for concepts to surpass your level of understanding. In fact, anticipate that to happen early on in the elementary years. When this happens, you are learning right alongside your child, which models learning for your child. In the late middle school and high school years, hiring a tutor or enrolling your child in online or dual credit college courses are also an option.
- **How will I know what my child needs to know?** There are many tools to guide you. Seek direction from your co-ops and homeschool communities, use curriculum sets, or search online for direction based on your child's age.

However, the best gauge of what your child needs to know is based on where they are right now. In homeschooling, no one is "behind" or "ahead." Each child is learning right where they are, at their level.

- **What if my child grows up to be socially awkward?** In the public school system today, children are surrounded by technology and often have their nose in a tablet or some other device. Homeschool communities offer ample opportunities for socialization that are intergenerational and span a wide range of interests. Which do you think better encourages socialization? If you are seeking socialization, you will find it.
- **What if people think we are weird?** Some people will.
- **What if my neighbor calls the cops because I am not sending my kids to school?** When you decide to homeschool, look up the homeschool laws in your state. Learn what kind of records you need to keep and what requirements you need to meet each year. I would also recommend seeking membership with the Home School Legal Defense Association (HSLDA). They provide legal services to homeschool families if the need arises.
- **How in the world will we ever fill a day?** This was a huge fear of mine. Now I find myself

wishing there were more hours in the day. Between co-op, music lessons, scouts, church activities, and homeschool lessons, it doesn't take long for our days to fill up. I would caution against getting so busy that your family misses out on learning that can take place during boredom. Boredom is when play and adventures and discoveries happen.

o **What about sports?** With homeschooling on the rise, there are many communities offering organized sports teams specifically for homeschool students. If something like that is not offered in your area, check with your local public school. Depending on state law, most public schools allow homeschool students to participate in extracurricular activities such as sports, clubs, prom, etc.

o **What if my kids don't want to learn from me?** Some days they won't. Some days will be harder than others. You know your child better than anyone, and you know their abilities, their challenges, how they learn best, what they need, and when they need to take a break. Some days render a break, and some days are a great opportunity to talk through overcoming challenges and to "…do it heartily, as to the Lord…" (Colossians 3:23).

Every homeschool parent has fear. Fear of failure. Fear of messing up our kids. Fear of messing up their future. Pray about these fears. "I sought the Lord and he heard me, and delivered me from all my fears" (Psalm 34:4). You are embarking on a journey that has the potential for so much good. Good for both your child and you. Don't let Satan put fear in your heart and lie to you. Satan will tell you that you can't do it. That others are gifted to homeschool, but you are not. That you are not educated enough to educate your child. These are lies. You are your child's best teacher because you know your child and their capacity to learn better than anyone. You can do this!

4
Jesus. Yoga Pants. Homeschool.

Jesus. Yoga pants. Homeschool. In that order. This journey is so much easier with Jesus. When you follow God's calling in your life, you will be blessed. And on the frustrating days, stop and pray. Stop and pray with your child in the middle of the lesson. Pray for patience, for wisdom, for the ability to teach them in a way they can learn from. Pray for your child to have patience, to be calm, and to be receptive to learn during school time. It's amazing what taking a deep breath and praying can do in the middle of a school lesson seemingly at a head lock.

And those frustrating days will come. There are days I lust after the yellow school bus as it drives past my house. That fantasy of meeting my friends for breakfast has slipped away and been replaced with co-ops and curriculum swaps. Some days your kids won't want to learn from you. Some days they won't like school, and neither will you. Some days you will wonder why you are putting yourself through this, and if you are doing the right thing for your child.

On those days, remind yourself to "…not be weary in well doing…" (Galatians 6:9). Because you are doing something so fruitful, and you are doing it well. It is easy to feel weary in the thick of it, but ask God to rejuvenate your spirit. Ask for wisdom as a parent, and as a teacher. God may reveal that you need to engage in self-care or attend a homeschool conference to rejuvenate your attitude and give you fresh ideas. He may encourage you to try a different teaching technique that may resonate with your child more.

Or, He may lead you to take a break. As I write this, we are on a one month break from homeschooling. We are not even mentioning school for the entire month. Everyone needed a break. And I am using this break to revamp my teaching techniques and try a few new ideas once we resume next month. God restores us when we seek Him.

Yoga pants. I am most comfortable when I am wearing yoga pants. Not only do they feel great, they are just my style. Especially the wild patterned, colorful yoga pants. And that is what I wear while I'm at home teaching my children. I could mimic a traditional school setting by wearing a blue jean jumper with an apple embroidered on the pocket protector, but that is just not me. I jokingly mention this because it isn't uncommon for homeschool families to try and turn their home into a traditional school setting. Instead of letting school happen organically in the home setting, they want to turn their home into a mini school.

I was guilty of this. When we decided to homeschool, I suggested to my husband that we put the house on the market and look for a bigger home with an extra room. I could turn that room into a little classroom, because I needed a space in the house designated for school time. I needed to mount a flag on the wall. I needed bulletin boards with seasonal boarders. I needed desks. My husband gently reminded me that I didn't need all of that to teach our children. We were not going to change our home to revolve around school. School was going to fit into our home.

So momma, you do you. For me, that is yoga pants. It is also starting our day with breakfast and cartoons. It is getting out of the house each day, whether that be simply a trip to the grocery store or an educational outing to the library or science center. It is school for one to two hours per day, a few days a week. Sometimes our weeks get busy, and we school on Saturday. It is play. Lots and lots of play. It is God at the center of all we do. But it is *always* while wearing yoga pants.

Homeschooling is a journey that looks different for every family. Some families start at birth and homeschool through high school. Some homeschool during the elementary years before transitioning to private or public school. Some send their children to school during the younger years, and homeschool in high school. Some use workbooks. Some use online programs. Some use curriculum sets. Some mish mash together things they see on Pinterest. Some are very structured and scheduled throughout the day, everyday. Some take a nature journal outside and spend the day playing. Some are involved in every co-op and activity their community has to offer.

No journey is better or worse than another. Each family has to find out what works best for their lifestyle and their child's learning style. While it can be helpful to talk to other homeschool families and find out how others are doing it, don't feel like you have to fit into a certain mold. What works for others may not work for you, and vise versa. It is your homeschool. Make it your own, unique to your family's interests, passions, and quarks. Some families even name their homeschool. A friend of mine named their homeschool "Hogwarts" because her family loves Harry Potter. She even had a bumper sticker made for her vehicle that says "Hogwarts Honor Student." Build your school around your home, and have fun with it.

5
The Curriculum Quandary

The kneejerk response to making the decision to homeschool is commonly to rush out and buy a curriculum, or five. I am going to propose why this may not be the most effective first step and suggest other steps of action to help a new homeschooler, or seasoned homeschooler wanting to try a different tactic, to get started. Obviously, different ages will have some commonalities and some important differences, and I will touch on those. And as always, I encourage each homeschooler to mold their homeschool into their lives. Do what works for your family.

It makes sense to be interested in buying curriculum. It's like opening a brand new box of crayons on the first day of school. So many colors and options, and everything is bright and shiny and new. Curriculum sets can keep you organized and on track, and give you direction. Curriculum sets have been put together by intelligent people who know what they are talking about and know what a student around the age of my child should be working on. They have been organized to teach children how to learn things I may not know how to teach.

All of the above is true. Curriculum sets certainly have their benefits and their place. However, there are several reasons why buying a curriculum set shouldn't be your first step to homeschooling. First off, curriculum sets can be very expensive. It doesn't take long to have hundreds or sometimes thousands of dollars in your shopping cart. While some of these curriculum sets are worth every penny, you don't yet know which curriculum set is the best fit for your teaching style, your child's learning style, and your life.

Beginning the homeschool journey involves a lot of trial and error. Does my child seem to learn best from a workbook, a video, a computer program, or a hands-on lesson taught by me? Does my child need lots of repetition and practice, or do they get frustrated with driving in the same point over and over? Based on my child's attention span, what will our daily time commitment to school be? What other activities is my child involved in that might contribute to their learning experience? What does my child already know? What is my child struggling in?

In addition to taking the time to explore what learning experience will be most beneficial to your child, consider what teaching experience will be the best fit for you. What subjects do you feel confident teaching yourself? What subjects would you prefer to use the aid of workbooks, computer, or video? Are there any subjects you feel the need to hire an external person to help teach your child, such as music or art? What does your average day look like and how much time will you be able to dedicate to teaching your child?

A downside to curriculum sets is they are often based around an age or academic level, and after you have spent hundreds of dollars on these sets, you flip through them and realize your child isn't on track with some or much of it. Your child may be advanced in certain areas, not ready for certain areas, and right on target with the rest. You may find yourself only utilizing a third of the curriculum set, improvising on the rest, or worse, spending more money on other curriculums to fill in the gaps.

The great thing about homeschooling, and this may feel uncomfortable for those of us used to the public school system, is no one is behind. So, while it is helpful to have a guide as to what other children around the age of my child are learning at this time, don't let that put pressure on you. While setting goals for yourself and letting your child set goals for themselves is great, allow some flexibility. Your child is where they are, and that is where you meet them.

6
Step One: Community

There is no reason to be a trail blazer when there are many homeschool parents that have gone before you to make the mistakes and tell you what they've learned. A community of homeschoolers has many benefits. The first is exactly what it is, community. In any life journey, doing it with others always makes the road more enjoyable. A community of homeschool mommas will likely become some of your closest friends. Mainly because you are in the same trenches together.

Don't get me wrong, I have many friends that are not homeschoolers and are dear, dear friends of mine. But to be honest, there is an entire part of my life they frankly just don't get. Sure, they may respect my choices and even applaud me for the sacrifice I am making, but they don't truly understand what being a homeschool family is. Also, our schedules look very different. They may want their kids to play with your kids in the evenings or on weekends when they are out of school, whereas we have been socializing throughout our weekdays through homeschool programs and co-ops and the evenings and weekends are strictly family time. Or, summer time might be considered free time for them because they are out of school, but we keep somewhat of a summer school schedule to retain our learning and allow for year 'round flexibility.

Fellow homeschool parents get it. While every homeschool family does things differently, there is a comradery in the fact that each of you are doing things differently. Having a community of homeschool friends means friends for you, parents who are like minded in the area of school and potentially other convictions, and who can relate to the joys and struggles of schooling your child at home. Because the joys of homeschooling are huge, and it is great to share those joys and small victories with people who understand. And the struggles of homeschooling are real, and it is healthy to vent those struggles and brainstorm possible solutions with a person who also experiences homeschool struggles and whose first suggestion won't be, "maybe everyone would benefit from going to public school." While a valid suggestion at times, it can feel very defeating when the only suggestion a non-homeschool friend or family member can give you is to give up.

Having a community of homeschool friends also means friends for your child. This is very important. One of the first concerns mentioned when discussing homeschooling is socialization. Socialization is important, but the public school system is not the only way to be socialized. Homeschooling today offers so many opportunities for students to be social. If you know any homeschoolers in your area, ask them what organizations are offered for homeschool students. If you don't know any homeschoolers in your area, try Google searching or searching on social media for homeschool groups in your area. Results will vary based on the area you live in.

When we lived in a small midwestern community, there were two homeschool programs/co-ops that met in a nearby town. We joined one of those co-ops and immediately had a community of friends, for both myself and my children, with whom we could exchange ideas and live life with. This particular co-op met one morning a week and offered my children a time of group learning and group play they were not able to get at home. Now that we live in a moderate size town, there are a handful of homeschool programs/co-ops to choose from and several extracurricular programs and field trip groups. We have dabbled in all of them and love the variety each offers.

I am a strong advocate for joining a weekly homeschool program or co-op. It will round out your homeschool experience not only for your child, but for you as well. There are certain aspects of education that are much better learned in a group setting, such as public speaking, discussing differing ideas, or learning to collaborate and work together. But more importantly, it will become your community. Your people.

While being a homeschool family is a niche in itself, modern-day homeschoolers are quick to label themselves by what type of homeschool model they identify with. Common models include Classical, Charlotte Mason, and Unschooling. While I am not going to explain what each of these models entail, I would encourage you to research the different homeschool models to see what interests you. However, don't feel that you need to choose one and fit into that box. You may find it beneficial to use parts from each, avoid parts from each, and piece together what works for you. Similarly, I would caution against writing off homeschool programs or co-ops because they don't identify with your model. Try out what your community has to offer, then decide which programs or co-ops best compliment and round out your homeschool.

7
Step Two: Creating YOUR Homeschool

Once you find a community of homeschoolers to be a part of, bounce ideas off of, and learn about their journey which will help you on your journey, the next step is to make a plan. Write this plan in pencil, because beginning a homeschool journey is trial and error. In fact, with each passing year as our children grow and learn and change, homeschooling is always trial and error. But you will want to make a plan to guide you and give you direction, even if that plan is very fluid.

Making this plan is kind of like making a mosaic. There will be many pieces that form your finished product. The first step is to find out what students your child's age are learning in public school. Before you freak out, hear me out. I know homeschool is not public school. However, it is helpful to know what students your child's age are learning. The easiest way to find this out is simply to Google search "what does a child in X grade learn?" As you read through the results, take note of what your child already knows how to do, what they are in the process of mastering, and what they have not yet learned. There may be some things you disagree with, and if so, don't put those things on your list. There may be some things not listed, but you find important and want to add to your list. Then add them to your list.

I also recommend you Google search a grade or two below your child and a grade or two ahead of your child. The beauty of homeschooling is your child may be the age of a public school first grader, but reading at a third grade level yet working on kindergarten math principles. Researching what children are learning a grade or two ahead and below will help you realize any subjects you may have skipped over or still need to work on, and will help you move forward with your child if they are ready to move on in certain subjects.

This is also a great time to talk with your homeschool community. You might hear new ideas like teaching cursive before you teach printing, or delaying certain subjects and focusing more on play, or introducing a foreign language. All of these tidbits of knowledge are helping you form your plan.

Look at this list of possible learning objectives you are compiling, and think of your child. How do they learn best? What are they ready for? What will challenge them? What will frustrate them and may need to be taught in a different way? In addition to academic objectives, are there any non-academic skills you would like to work on? This can be anything from integrating chores into your daily routine, to teaching life skills such as cooking, cleaning, balancing a checkbook, or serving in a ministry at your church. All of these things make up your mosaic of a school plan.

Look at this list and choose some goals for your school year. Again, write these goals in pencil, as they will likely change. You may find one of your goals are reached within a month or so because you had no idea your child would catch onto that math concept so quickly. Or you may find you set a goal too high, and you need to take a couple steps back and set a different goal. You may add goals throughout the year as your child develops new interests, such as music, art, drama, or a foreign language. It is not what is on your plan that matters, only that you have a plan and give yourself and your child grace and flexibility to change it if need be.

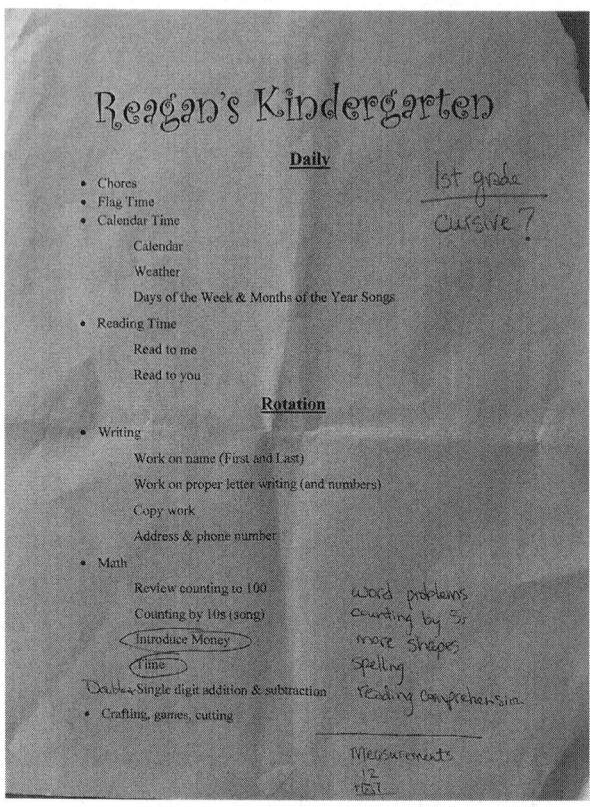

This plan was taped to the inside of our homeschool cupboard, which is a kitchen cabinet I emptied out to make a place to store all of our homeschool materials. As you can see, this plan was altered several times throughout the kindergarten year.

Once you have this pencil written plan, ask yourself what tools you need to help your child learn the objectives involved. Depending on the age or level of your child, you may realize you don't need a curriculum to meet some academic goals. I am personally not a fan of curriculum sets until around middle school. I believe many elementary learning objectives can be met with household items such as paper, writing utensils, buttons, glue, scissors, paint, magnets, blocks, food, kitchen supplies, water and books. If you need elementary workbooks or other supplementary materials, I recommend shopping at the Dollar Tree.

Friends, the Dollar Tree. It is the best kept secret in homeschooling. There are some learning materials sold at homeschool conventions for fifty dollars that I have bought near replicas of at the Dollar Tree. Everything from maps, construction paper, beginner's writing paper, arts and craft supplies, cursive writing workbooks, flash cards, bulletin board pin ups, stickers, math workbooks, reading books, awards, I'm telling you it's amazing!

Once you have the tools you need, you may be able to teach your elementary student how to read, write, and do basic math without a curriculum set. However, if you need the structure and assistance of a curriculum set, by all means purchase one. There is something about following a curriculum guide that helps you stay on track and feel like you have a plan. But I do want to empower and encourage you. You know how to read. You know how to write. You know how to do basic math. You can teach your child to do these things. If you need some direction, Youtube videos (for you, not your child) can help you get on your way. What I'm saying is, you don't have to take out a small loan to homeschool. You can do a lot without curriculum.

Using construction paper, marker, and buttons
to practice sorting and classifying.

Once your child is in middle school and high school, curriculum can be so helpful. There may be learning objectives you do not feel comfortable to teach, or let's be honest, we don't remember some of this stuff ourselves so we will be learning right alongside our child. And depending on the subject, curriculum does not stop at books. Today there are resources available to homeschool students offering a variety of instruction such as videos and online courses. Your child can also enroll in online college classes and begin earning college credit.

No matter the age of your student or whether or not you are being guided by curriculum, make sure your plan includes reading time. Reading time is probably the most important part of our day. It consists of early readers reading aloud or mature readers reading to themselves, but most importantly, it consists of me reading aloud to my children. No matter their age. This may sound strange if you have high school age children, but it is immensely beneficial regardless of age.

However, I am going to let you in on a secret. While reading happens everyday in our home, I have never referred to recreational reading as part of school. I have always set the tone that reading is something we enjoy doing, both independently and as a family. I don't want to label recreational reading as anything other than an activity we do for enjoyment. I believe that framing reading in this positive way encourages reading that is intrinsically motivated.

Remember that the Bible can be an amazing homeschool resource. The Bible in and of itself can be used as a guide to an academic year. Starting in the first chapter of Genesis, you can discuss science subjects such as astronomy, classification of plants and animals, and anatomy. As subjects are covered in the Bible, use certain topics as a springboard for questions and further discoveries. Use scripture to practice handwriting. Use the Bible as your read-aloud book for one of your academic years. For elementary age children, I highly recommend the *Jesus Storybook Bible* by Sally Lloyd-Jones. For middle and high school age children, any study Bible will work. The topics for discussion are endless in the Bible, and your child will be learning biblical lessons alongside their academic lessons.

8
Step Three: The Home-Field Trip Balance

Your child's learning does not have to be limited to your academic objectives or co-op activities. Homeschooling opens up your child's schedule to have the time to enjoy extracurricular activities they may not have had the time for if they were in public school, or they may have made time for them but their schedule was packed so tight there wasn't time to breath. Since homeschooling requires many less hours than public school, that time can be used to explore a wide variety of interests. This can include extracurriculars such as sports, the arts, scouting, or volunteering. This can also include fun field trips.

A field trip can be as simple as a weekly trip to your local library. No matter the age of your child, I recommend a weekly trip to the library. If your child has not yet learned to read, participating in story times offered by your library will help develop their love for reading and a mindset that reading is fun. Also, your nonreader can simply flip through books and look at the pictures. Get your child their own library card and let them take ownership of checking out books of interest to them each week.

For those with older children, weekly trips to the library allow your child to check out books that interest them and encourage reading. They may also look into books that help them write a paper they are working on or learn more about a subject they are learning. Spend some time at the library perusing the book shelves and reading, and then encourage your child to check out books to read throughout the week. You can also use this time to find books that support what you are teaching that week, or books you would like to use for read-aloud time.

Depending on the size of your town, additional field trips can vary. Larger cities may offer museums, science centers, zoos, children's museums, art galleries, aquariums, or nature centers. If you live in a city like this, you are living in a homeschooler's dream land. Take advantage of it. Field trips make learning come alive.

Use your discretion as to how much you want field trip learning experiences to be organic or if you want to be intentional with field trip related assignments. For younger children, I would encourage you to let learning be as organic as possible. Let them explore and have fun.

On the ride home, ask them what their favorite part was, but try not to turn the day into a school lesson. Field trips are a part of school, without your child knowing they are learning.

For older children, organic learning is still encouraged, but you may want to mix in some intentional assignments. For example, if they are learning about a certain time period in history and take a field trip to the art museum, ask your child to keep their eye out for pieces of art created during the time period they are studying. You may ask them to write a reflection piece on the work of art and how it related to what they are learning about that particular time in history.

If you do not live in a big city offering these kinds of educational opportunities, I feel your pain. We have yet to live in a big city. However, Google searching and asking around your homeschool community will often result in finding fun field trip opportunities that are day trip worthy. And if these day trips can be done with your community of homeschoolers, even better. Or family weekend getaways and family vacations may be when your best field trips happen. I am not suggesting family time revolves around school. Family vacations should be about making great memories, eating delicious food, and spending time together. But if a family vacation happens to be near a NASA Space Station or the White House, by all means, call that a homeschool win-win.

But in between those trips, find learning opportunities in your small town. Maybe you live near a farm you could visit and learn about milking a cow, planting, or large animal care. Or perhaps you live near an Amish community that builds handcrafted furniture without the use of power tools. If nothing else, I encourage you to enjoy nature. Go to the park, go on walks, keep a nature journal, just be outdoors. Being outside, and away from technology, is the perfect place to get your child's imagination and creative juices flowing.

When homeschooling, find a healthy balance between being at home and getting out of the house. It is easy to fall heavy on one end of that spectrum. Some families may prefer being home more, finding it difficult to meet their educational objectives each day when they venture out. They may feel that field trips are getting in the way of their goals. But realize that field trips can help you meet your goals, in addition to making learning something your child can experience instead of just read about. Field trips can also be social, and you may find that some wonderful family memories are made. Allow your school schedule some flexibility for field trips.

On the other hand, some families prefer to be on the go. They may love field trips and social gatherings so much they have no problem being flexible and putting their school schedule on hold for fun and educational events that pop up. I can completely relate to this, because I am a social butterfly and thrive in community. However, realize that sometimes you have to be *home* in order to *homeschool*. Being at home allows you to focus on educational objectives, gives time for reading and writing, and gives time to just be still. In a world where we are always busy and on the go, giving your child opportunities to be still is a gift. They don't need to be stimulated and entertained all the time. They need to learn how to be bored, how to let their mind rest, and how to enjoy quiet time.

Find that healthy balance for your homeschool. You may need to make a weekly or monthly calendar to help you find a good mix of co-op, field trips, and home time. Also, never underestimate the use of car time. Time spent in the car does not need to be wasted time. In fact, some of my homeschool friends would say their best learning happens in the car. Some homeschool programs and curriculum sets use songs as a part of their teaching strategies. Play those songs in the car. Read-aloud time can also happen in the car with audio books. Or use car time to review math facts, quiz your child, or simply talk about discoveries you make while driving down the road.

The only thing I will tell you NOT to do in the car, is turn on a movie or hand your child a device. Even if you are not doing any formal education in the car through read-aloud or memory work, just talk to your child. Or don't talk. Allow them to look out the window at the world around them and be alone with their thoughts. But chalking up car time as time wasted will only waste time. That time can be so valuable as long as a device doesn't steal the opportunity.

9
Exposure Learning

My favorite homeschool method is something I call Exposure Learning. Exposure Learning consists of exposing your child to learning opportunities throughout your home in a very intentional yet organic way. This wasn't natural to me at first because I am an OCD neat freak who likes everything to be put back in its place and counter spaces bare and clean. But I started realizing that when learning materials were left out, my children would go back to them throughout the day to further explore.

Exposure learning can look several different ways, but I want to give you some examples. No matter the age of your child, give them exposure to age appropriate books in your home. Garage sale or go to thrift stores to start building your library. Depending on the age of your child, these can range from picture books, chapter books, fiction, non-fiction, encyclopedias, text books, reference books, and Bibles. Always be growing your library. And of course, books will be coming and going on a weekly basis due to your weekly trips to the local library.

Give your child exposure to concepts they are learning through wall hangings. The more your child sees an idea, the more familiar they will be with it. If they are only looking at an idea during school hours, then putting everything away, you are limiting their exposure. Many things your child is learning can be made into some sort of visual or poster and hung on the wall for exposure every time it is looked at or walked by. Especially if you have a visual learner, just looking at a visual will help them retain the information they are exposed to. Exposure Learning gives your child so many more opportunities to learn, and can make learning organic and fun.

Jesus. Yoga Pants. Homeschool.

An example of Exposure Learning. Homemade wall hanging to encourage learning money concepts. When teaching money, I recommend using real money. Play money is often inaccurate in its size and appearance, which can lead to confusion when your child is introduced to real money.

If they are learning geography, hang maps on the wall. If they are learning the anatomy of a plant or animal, hang a labeled poster on the wall. As your child is learning their numbers and ABCs, hang them on the wall. If they are learning the solar system, make a mobile and hang it from their bedroom ceiling. If they are working on spelling words or a foreign language, make flashcards and hang them with their respectable objects around the house. Leave math manipulatives and games out so they can be picked up and played with and explored anytime. Put plastic measuring cups and spoons in the bathtub as bath toys. Use refrigerator magnets for learning colors, numbers, and letters. Leave a sand tray on the kitchen table so your child can practice writing their letters and numbers anytime the urge hits them. Always have creativity supplies out or handy, like paper, crayons, scissors, stickers, and glue.

While it is tempting to get this giant keyboard out of my kitchen, leaving it out encourages my daughter to practice her music lesson without me having to ask. Also, notice the homemade wall hangings in the background that encourage counting to 100 and skip counting by twos.

A homemade sand tray can easily be made using a baking dish with a layer of salt at the bottom. This is a fun, sensory way for children to practice their letters and numbers. Another variation of this is to spread a layer of whipped cream on a cookie sheet. Same idea, only messier.

Homeschooling isn't about your child becoming a genius, it's about teaching your child how to learn and love learning. If electronic devices are off and your child is exposed to books, learning tools, and creative materials, they will learn how to use their time to learn. And they will learn to love learning.

When asked how many hours per day I dedicate to homeschooling, I often say, "We school all day long, but not at all." What I mean is some days we are not doing any formal book work or introduction of new ideas. Sometimes I simply set math manipulatives on the coffee table, games on the kitchen table, playdough and crafting materials on the kids' table, measuring cups and spoons in the water table on our back deck, and set out a few new books. With the tv off, these simple exposures make for a great day of playing, exploring, and learning.

If the idea of mobiles, posters, and flashcards hanging all over the walls of your home is giving you anxiety, you're in good company. Remember, this is your homeschool. Do what fits for you. For me, the walls around the kids' table are school walls. Those walls expose my children to all sorts of educational information. And the kids' table is where most of our schooling at home happens. So, you can stop twitching now. I don't have a flag pole installed in our living room for the morning pledge each day, and there are no bulletin boards with seasonal borders hanging on our walls. Our home looks quite normal and homey, with a very educational kids' table.

Jesus. Yoga Pants. Homeschool.

This kids' table is where most of our formal schooling takes place. My children will often gravitate toward this area throughout the day to "play" with the manipulatives, puzzles, or games I leave out. I rotate these things frequently to keep learning new and exciting.

10
Scheduling and Structure

There is definitely a time and place for schedules and structure. I don't want to come across as a kumbaya homeschooler that suggests just letting your child run around outside all day long and that is all they need. But I also don't want to come across as a drill sergeant homeschooler that has every minute of the day scheduled beginning with a 5:00am wake up time. Like anything else in life, find balance somewhere in the middle.

My recommendation is to have very little scheduling and structure for preschool age children, and slowly and gradually build a schedule and structure year by year. The elementary years should consist of a lot of play, because that is how younger children learn about the world around them. There are ways younger children can learn about structure without having every minute of their day scheduled. Children can quickly pick up on your family's everyday living schedule. Keeping a consistent family schedule will help your younger child learn what scheduling and structure is all about. For example, a general time of day when everyone in the home is waking up, keeping consistent meal times, and keeping consistent nap/rest times and bedtimes. Children thrive with consistency, and these basic consistencies in your home will prepare them for further structure as they get older.

Elementary students, while still needing lots of free time and play time for creativity and imaginative play, can be introduced to more consistent homeschool scheduling. Depending on the age of your elementary age student and their development, I recommend one to two hours of structured learning time. This can look many different ways depending on your homeschool methods, but learning to set and accomplish daily educational goals will help your child get used to structured learning time. As their reading skills improve and they gain confidence in reading, writing, and mathematics, they will also learn to be self-led learners and take the initiative to fulfill daily goals without as much prompting from you as when they were younger.

Jesus. Yoga Pants. Homeschool.

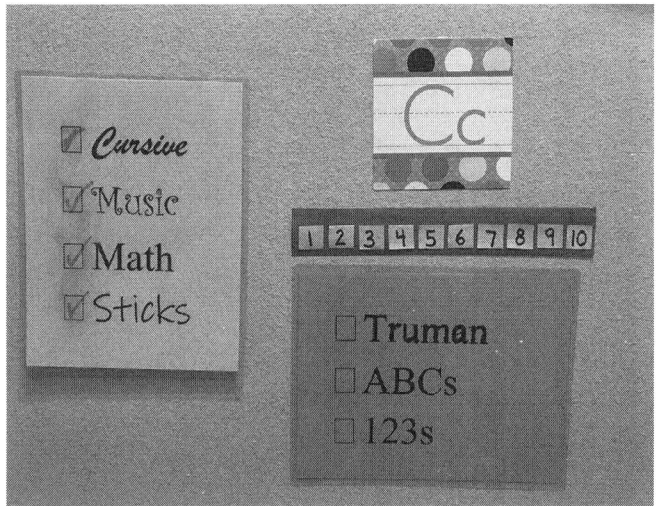

An example of daily goals for preschool and elementary age children. "Sticks" is simply writing learning concepts on popsicle sticks. Everyday we draw one stick, and that is what we work on. For example, "time," "money," "measurements," "spelling," or "flash cards." These are concepts you may not want to review every day, but covering them once a week at random keeps learning fun.

As your child progresses through middle school and high school, time spent schooling will increase some, and scheduling and structure will become much more important. However, your child is also becoming more self-sufficient and learning becomes much more independent. Your role as a one-on-one teacher backs up to more of a support and guidance role. It is important your child learns personal responsibility for completing tasks and practices time management.

One complication with homeschooling middle school and high school students is the tendency for them to want to sleep in. Their bodies are developing and growing and requiring more sleep, and it can be tempting to sleep until noon. You know your child best and what schedule works best for your family, but keep in mind you are preparing your child for college and/or the work force. Learning to be up at a certain time to begin various responsibilities will help them in the future. Your middle and high school student most likely will have chores, school responsibilities, family responsibilities, church responsibilities, and possibly a job. It will be difficult to accomplish those responsibilities well if half of the day is spent in bed.

While you will be creating your own structure and schedule, you will have freedom from following a traditional school schedule. When your child is progressing in a subject, you can keep on moving forward with them. When your child is struggling in a subject, you can stay there for as long as they need until they are ready to move forward. School doesn't have to start around Labor Day and end around Memorial Day. It doesn't have to be Monday through Friday. And if you consider your child to be in a certain "grade," that grade can start anytime. A homeschool friend of mine shared a photo of her daughter's first day of first grade. It was a random day in the middle of April.

Give yourself permission to take breaks when needed. Taking breaks can sometimes be what leads to a learning breakthrough. If you find your child is getting so frustrated with a subject that they are beginning to loath that subject, or it is causing them self-worth issues because they struggle to move forward, take a break. Pushing forward will just make the negative feelings continue to amp up, and the goal is not to cause harm. Sometimes taking a break, letting that part of your child's brain rest for a period of time (weeks, maybe even months), and then slowly reintroducing the concept in a fresh manner can result in a learning breakthrough. Also, consider that every child develops academically at different speeds and in different ways. With time, a concept may click with your child simply because their brain developed to the point that it was ready to master that concept.

11
Homeschooling Your High Schooler

While I have not yet experienced homeschooling a high schooler, I have some insight on preparing a high school student for college. Before embarking on my homeschool journey, I held several positions at a midwestern university including Mental Health Counselor, Coordinator of the First-Year Experience, Academic Advisor and Adjunct Instructor teaching Psychology, Career and Life Planning, and Freshman Orientation. The knowledge I gleaned from working with college students, in addition to the years I spent in college earning my bachelors, masters, and doctoral degrees, have influenced the way I will approach the high school years and college preparedness.

I can still hear my doctoral professors' words, "Always be reading, and always be writing." This advice is the key to knowledge and the venue toward compiling thoughts. I would give this same advice to those homeschooling a high schooler. At the top of your homeschool goals should be reading and writing.

I'm not going to tell you what your child should be reading, but there are many great resources out there to help you choose. Of course, the Bible is a great read, continuously. There are also books and online resources, such as Sarah Mackenzie's *Read-Aloud Revival*, solely on the topic of what books are recommended to read at each age or developmental level. Your local library is always a great resource for book lists and recommendations. My favorite place to find great American literature is the thrift store. In fact, no matter what age your child is, if you ever find some of the old classics at the thrift store, snatch them up. Libraries are carrying less and less of the great books we were raised on, and are replacing them with more recent publications. Recent relevance is taking the place of award winning literature. Historical literature is a great window into a time different than the one we live in today. Give your child the opportunity to read some of these greats!

Writing topics can come from their readings, current events, historical events, or really anything encouraging critical thinking. In fact, I will go as far as to say that critical thinking is the number one most important skill your child can learn. After four years of undergraduate studies and six years of graduate work, I can't tell you all of the tidbits of knowledge I have memorized and forgotten, but I do know how to think on my own. Thinking on your own is an invaluable skill many will never develop. Today's generations have become quite good at doing what they are told, without even knowing why or bothering to ask. Teach your child to ask questions. Teach your child to consider both sides of an argument, researching both as unbiased as possible while still through the lens of their values, and defend their stance.

When your child is old enough, give them controversial topics and a deadline to present what they learned about both sides, and where they stand based on their findings and values. Controversial topic ideas include abortion, vaccines, political affiliation, school, religion, gay marriage, etc. (Note: Encouraging your child to research controversial topics such as these should be reserved for mature late high school students. Their stance may not always line up with yours, but it is important for them to explore their ideas on controversial topics within the guidance of your home before they are introduced first hand to many of these topics in college or the work place).

One Sunday I was volunteering in our church nursery. I was serving alongside a seasoned homeschool mom of four, her oldest being of middle school age. She was expressing her concerns to me of whether she was "doing enough." We began discussing what we, as educated homeschool moms, felt was really important for our children to know. This is what we decided, and I stand by this list still today: It is important for our children to enjoy reading and read often, knowing how to seek information and answer questions. It is important for our children to be able to express themselves, both verbally and in written form. It is important for our children to be able to perform basic math concepts, including how to count change back. It is important that our children know how to work, value work, and have a strong work ethic. And most importantly, our children need critical thinking skills.

That's it. After all my years in academia, this is what I believe the tools of success are. Now, I am not saying you can throw out your curriculum guides and kick your feet up. In fact, the focus on reading can be integrated into learning subjects such as history, science, civics, etc. What I am saying is I wouldn't worry so much about your child memorizing and mastering every subject in their textbooks. Think big picture. Focus more on giving your child the tools to be successful, as you are fostering their spiritual growth, character, morals, and values.

In addition to your personal homeschool regimen, once your child is old enough to work, I strongly believe some of our best life-applicable learning happens through work experience. This can start when your child is in middle school if they show the maturity and drive for small entrepreneurial ventures such as babysitting, dog walking, or lawn care. Once they are of working age, a part-time job will teach them more life skills than any amount of book work ever could. Encourage them to seek out a part-time job that includes customer service, working with money, and ideally learning a skill. Unpaid apprenticeships or internships are another great way to learn a skill or discover a potential career path.

A concern many homeschool parents have is how their child will fare on the ACT. Homeschool students often are not as accustomed to standardized testing as public school students are. In addition, today's public schools often teach for the tests. Teaching for the test is not something commonly practiced in homeschooling, but in the case of the ACT, that may be exactly the approach to take. I have heard of homeschool families that, when ACT time was approaching, took a complete break from their usual school subjects, and solely studied the ACT.

If you have been teaching your homeschool student how to learn, they can learn how to take the ACT. There are ACT prep classes your child can take, there are ACT prep books, there are practice tests available, and the great thing about the ACT is you can take it as many times as you need to without penalty. Colleges will never know how many times you took it or your scores unless you request to submit your scores to them.

While many public schools are teaching for the tests, they are not necessarily teaching for college success. College is not about busy work and assembly line school days. College has a lot of flexibility, with most students taking two to four classes per day, and the rest of the day left completely up to them on how they spend it. There are very few deadlines throughout a semester, but often a major paper or exam at the end that should be prepared for independently throughout the entire semester. College is about reading and writing. No one will ask if you are keeping up with your reading, they will just assume you are. But the truth will come out in your writings and in your exams.

With that picture of college in mind, plan your child's high school homeschool years to prepare them. Always be reading and writing. Give them a deadline for a paper, exam, or project, but give them flexibility with their time to see how they spend it. And teach them to learn the ACT like they would learn any other subject.

Homeschool is the perfect environment for college readiness. However, not all students are ready for college at the age of eighteen. In fact, not all students are meant to go to college. While college used to be something for the few, it is now expected for most. Talk to your child about their post-high school aspirations. If they have a career path they are set on, and are ready to pursue that with everything they've got, then go for it.

If your child is unsure about their future or is interested in a trade not requiring college, I would caution against pushing them into college. College is not cheap, and it does not take long to wrack up student debt that can follow your child around until they are nearing retirement. Help your child look at the big picture as they are making post-high school decisions. Non-college options include learning a trade, exploring career opportunities through internships or apprenticeships, or getting an entry level job. A close family friend of ours didn't go the college route, and instead got a job as a cart pusher at a successful retailer. He now has a corporate position with that same retailer and provides for his family very well. The recipe for success does not always include college.

12
A Word of Encouragement

You got this. You can do this! You will never regret spending an extra year or two or twelve with your child. You will never say, "I wish I would have sent him away for the better part of each day so someone else could have invested in his life." No matter how great and kind a school teacher is, there is no one on this Earth that cares for your child as much as you do. There is no one more personally invested in your child as you are. No one wants to see them succeed more than you do.

Just getting started is the hardest part. The laundry list of fears will continue to grow until you surrender to them and give it a try. Once you do, I promise you the list will dissolve. Of course, challenges will arise, but having a strong foundation in why you are going down this road will help you take a deep breath and keep pressing forward. Lean on the Lord. He didn't call you to this journey and then leave you. He is with you every step of the way. But He also didn't promise it would be a cake walk. If homeschooling were easy, everyone would be doing it.

But you are not alone! You are amongst a growing community of parents that are choosing to homeschool, despite the challenges, because of the rewards. Seek out your community of homeschool families to build you up when you feel yourself getting knocked down. It is so much easier to get through a tough day when you know you are not alone on this journey. When your school day has hit a wall and you are ready to pull your hair out, know that there are many others with you in those trenches. Somedays I am nursing a baby while trying to teach my daughter cursive on a table that my son is dancing on while wearing only his underwear.

When my energy is running low, my ideas are getting boring and need refreshed, and I simply need reminded why I am doing this, my favorite thing to do is attend a homeschool conference. I find myself in a room of hundreds of parents that have made the same decision as we did to homeschool. We listen to speakers, buy resources and curriculums, and exchange ideas and encouragement. I attend these conferences partly to learn some new techniques and ideas, but mostly to get pumped up! Sometimes my homeschool spirit needs revived! But no matter what new ideas and inspirations

I learn at these conferences, every year I leave feeling like the common take away theme was this: Calm down.

Calm down. Think of the big picture. Keep it simple. You aren't going to mess up your kids. You are making the right decision. Keep at the forefront of your mind why you are doing this, and what is important. Follow where Jesus is leading you, put on some yoga pants, and homeschool.

About the Author

Dr. Natalie Trent Bruce was raised in Branson, Missouri. She earned a Bachelor's in Psychology from Truman State University in Kirksville, Missouri in 2005. She then earned a Master's in Counseling from the University of Missouri-Kansas City in 2007 and a Doctorate in Educational Leadership and Policy Analysis from the University of Missouri-Columbia in 2014. Her career in higher education began as a Mental Health Counselor and Academic Advisor for a midwestern university. As she began doctoral work, her sights were set on leadership within higher education administration. She was named the Coordinator of the First-Year Experience, in addition to being an Adjunct Instructor teaching Psychology, Career and Life Planning, and Freshman Orientation.

She met her husband, Travis, in 2004 and they were married in 2008. Her identity in the Lord has been shaped through becoming a mother and valuing her role as a wife and full-time homeschooling mom of their three children: Reagan, Truman, and Ingrid. She has a heart for mothers as they are finding their way in their motherhood journey. She enjoys speaking on subjects related to motherhood, including Postpartum Depression, pregnancy loss, joy in motherhood, and homeschooling. To contact Dr. Natalie Trent Bruce with questions or to schedule her as a speaker, contact her at:

www.drhomeschoolmom.com
nataliebruce@drhomeschoolmom.com